Activities We Do

We Make a Garden

by Connor Stratton

FOCUS READERS
SCOUT

www.focusreaders.com

Focus Readers is distributed by North Star Editions:
sales@northstareditions.com | 888-417-0195

Produced for Focus Readers by Red Line Editorial.

Photographs ©: ESB Professional/Shutterstock Images, cover, 1; SolStock/iStockphoto, 4; PeopleImages/iStockphoto, 7 (top), 16 (top right); stockphoto mania/Shutterstock Images, 7 (bottom); gorillaimages/Shutterstock Images, 9, 16 (bottom right); PavelRodimov/iStockphoto, 11; Ton Weerayut Photographer/Shutterstock Images, 13 (top); sturti/iStockphoto, 13 (bottom), 16 (bottom left); grki/iStockphoto, 15 (top); oneShutter oneMemory/Shutterstock Images, 15 (bottom); RomarioIen/iStockphoto, 16 (top left)

Library of Congress Cataloging-in-Publication Data
Names: Stratton, Connor, author.
Title: We make a garden / by Connor Stratton.
Description: Lake Elmo, MN : Focus Readers, [2020] | Series: Activities we do | Audience: Grades K to 3. | Includes index.
Identifiers: LCCN 2019016765 (print) | LCCN 2019011907 (ebook) | ISBN 9781641858007 (hardcover) | ISBN 9781641858694 (pbk.) | ISBN 9781641859950 (pdf) | ISBN 9781641859387 (ebook)
Subjects: LCSH: Gardening--Juvenile literature.
Classification: LCC SB457 .S85 2020 (ebook) | LCC SB457 (print) | DDC 635--dc23
LC record available at https://lccn.loc.gov/2019016765

Printed in the United States of America
Mankato, MN
May, 2019

About the Author

Connor Stratton enjoys working in the garden, eating popcorn, and watching movies with friends. He lives in Minnesota.

Table of Contents

shovel
soil

Gardening Is Fun

We make a garden.

We dig in the soil.

We use shovels.

We have **seedlings**.

We put them in the ground.

seedling

Caring for Plants

Plants need water.

We use a **watering can**.

We pour water onto

the plants.

watering can

Weeds grow in the garden.

We pull out the weeds.

We wear gloves.

weed
glove

Growing Food

Food grows in the garden.

Tomatoes grow in the garden.

Carrots grow in the garden.

tomato

carrots

We pick **berries**.

We eat the berries.

The berries taste good.

We had fun in the garden.

berry

Glossary

berries

seedlings

carrots

watering can

Index